LET'S TUNNEL AWAY

TWO HUNDRED POEMS BY

CHLOE PELLETIER

Printed by CreateSpace, An Amazon.com Company.
Available from Amazon.com, and other online stores.

First Edition 2016

Cover photo by Chloe Pelletier.
Cover and interior design by Cody Clarke.

The poems in this book were written from
October 22nd, 2014 to November 18th, 2016.

The author wishes to thank Cody Clarke
for his loving support during the writing process.

For Cody

Because my muse is in love with you.

1. Duct Tape
2. Conspiracy Theories
3. Baptism
4. First Cold Night of the Year
5. One Pair of Feet
6. Keeping Solid
7. Friendship
8. Reminisce
9. Being Ten Right Now
10. Legendary Place
11. Cooked
12. What If
13. Reminding of Drinking
14. Hands of Old
15. Moment Not Wanting
16. Itinerary
17. Glimpse a Silhouette
18. Uncomfortable Repeat
19. Diffused
20. Wiped
21. Invisible Man
22. Rescuing Selfishly
23. Stung
24. Motherhood
25. Dating Ad

101. Landfill

102. Infinite Women

103. Statue

104. Next Room Over

105. Warmth

106. Sticking

107. An Uncomfortable Night

108. Couch Jokings

109. Anticipating Fingertips

110. Checking In

111. Stepping Out

112. Upside Down

113. Skinny Fat

114. Comic Book Hair

115. Multiple Deaths Alone

116. Hopeful Sweater

117. Short Girl Glamour

118. Air Approaching

119. You Wake Me Up

120. Screen in Dark

121. Blank TV 2002 - 2016

122. Brushing Your Face

123. Your Own Love

124. As a Man

125. No People

Duct Tape

Friends like grandfathers
And grandfathers like friends
Hoping that never the conversation ends

Spaghetti upsets me
And delights me just the same

As does root beer and jerky
And kite flying and making

And jumping on hay
What is a windbreaker anyway

Conspiracy Theories

Something about APR financing
And limited times

Is repeated very quickly
Under the sound of the trickle of the faucet
Every time I rise

From the sensory deprivation
The water provides
My ears and eyes

Baptism

Slumping into bubbly steam
Body becomes pruney white
Flesh flaking off like corpses of the Titanic

A whale sinking half and half into the sea
Falling out and off of one's self like meat off a bone boiling

Eyes and ears and nose are plugged with two symmetrical hands
Desiring but also fearing to seep under

Congealing with tub and earth
And emerging in a new universe

Walking out as a fish
Ignorant of the filth of the bathwater

First Cold Night of the Year

Feet curl under blankets and under themselves
And when blankets and themselves curl no tighter

A ball is formed
Of tenseness and intensity
And sleeplessness

With exposed nose sticking out of it
Taking in crisp, clean, painful air

That reminds of many things
And causes tears that are warm
But sting when drying

Then retreating into the steam ball being built
Then gasping out again

And repeating this all night

One Pair of Feet

Some shoes are permanently glued
Not allowing bath or sleep
Without soap seeping
And dirt leaving

Some mornings are very cold
Joints stiffen as though old
And sun cannot penetrate
Only coffee and coconut oil
And reading things sent very late

There is only to eat and to move
And to move and to eat

To expand, to consume
Or else to worry
About never having relief or heat

Keeping Solid

Jeans holding legs up
And a braid holding the face up
To do anything

Like raid temples
Tend bar
Be on stage

Walk down the street
Keep the house clean

The only way to alleviate a constant headache
And constant stomach pain

Preferred over pajama slumping
And hair messery

Friendship

Go find the worms
Wriggling in the earth
And show me their tunnels
And let's comment on their squishy texture

As we bite off their heads
And observe their strange colors

Matte purple inside shiny pink
Only shit and sustenance
If it weren't for you and me

Reminisce

Tonight I am nothing but hunger and tiredness
The kind that microwaves potatoes
And covers them in whatever there is
And sleeps in between things
By accident

I'd like to think of something
Besides my needs

I'd like to think of something
Besides wanting

But I spent me earlier in the day

Being old temporarily is unpleasant
And makes me not look forward to what being old is

When I'm old I think I'll miss it
What it's like to not always feel like this

What was it like
To not always feel like this

Being Ten Right Now

The back of my throat is filling
With something like tears

And in my stomach I can feel it
And in my fears

And down in a pit
Where there isn't supposed to be
Anything there

Stuff that I deny existing
Is reaching up

And pulling forward
All of my hair

Legendary Place

A sprawl of deliciousness
Warm and red and yellow

In perspective, a landscape
Of fields and hills and meadows

And in a valley between two cliffs
There's a clearing with a gorge
Full of quicksand and mysteriousness
And vague scent of orange

A place where many men might explore
And like to put their face

As their minds echo porn
And hands surpass lace

Cooked

It starts in one place
Then spreads outward like oil in a pan

With it, flavors expand
From heat under them

And layers will be tasted
And colors seen
Red, yellow, and green

And eyes will shimmer
At one another

Like the sheen of the white
At the beginning

Tonight we will swim in cream

What If

If I'm wrong about everything
You, me, him, the future

At least there will still be everything
At least there will still be a universe

And weather
And water

But even that could falter
Even those could go

And so, there is only now
And to do what little I know

To take steps through the snow

Reminding of Drinking

Spilling water feels good sometimes
When it runs down your chin
And droplets trickle to find
Places to absorb on my dress

And there's no need to dry it off
The temperature in here is fine

There's no need to be alarmed
It isn't as though it's wine

Hands of Old

There was a time
With long hands on women
With narrow nails more like rectangles or ovals than squares

With knuckles so prominent they actually existed
Instead of mere dimples in plump flesh

And wrinkles in between existed
And lines and pores, not just flat

And colors
Pink and purple and linen

And no needs for manicures
To compensate for lack of all that

Moment Not Wanting

The warm and toasty shadows
With crumbs on their edge

Do not surround a gallows
But instead, shelves and beds

The feeling of sleeves on too-warm arms
And bellies well-fed

And for once, no fear of harm
It's gone, I'll sleep instead

Quickly, please place your head outside
While the cold feels good

Place your head outside and say to anybody
We're done, we've gone to bed

Itinerary

Treat it like it's a hotel
Like you're on vacation

Do not allow yourself to be under the spell
Do not accept your placement

Discern the location you are in
With the eyes of a patron

Move quickly as though catching a flight
And spend no hours wasted

Glimpse a Silhouette

A good cold outside
Like a glass of water

And as you walk a good alone
With fresh air in your lungs
But plenty of warmth in your chest and stomach

You see a cat crossing the road
As quickly as they can do it

With paws that barely touch the ground
But to sprint, it refuses

And as you call and inch forever closer
Her eyes begin to glow

And when you could just barely touch her
Again, off she goes

Uncomfortable Repeat

Little toe snags on hole once made by opposite big
At the most inopportune time which is always

Make note to throw away these socks
As they are a blight to sanity

But never do and never sew
As sewing would take so long
And make me think of sad things

And so I keep snagging and forgetting
Until my toe breaks or something

Diffused

Early morning, cool but warm
Under a cover there's breathing

And I can see the colors under your skin
And the flecks in your eyes
And the pinks in your cheeks and your grin

I can see your tears shimmering
As the melatonin leaves your brain
And I can see the blood green in your veins

My hair falling on your hair
Framing your face

Twisting with yours into brown and black rope
A neural pathway, electric with sunlight

Forehead to forehead
Maintaining this moment

Of me sitting on top of you
In shared memory for all time

Wiped

Coffee flowing through me in the workplace
Like a team doing a fast clean
As an assembly line

Making my veins feel
Like one of those slippery things
Filled with glitter
Getting squeezed

About to fly out of my hands
And bounce on the tile

Almost exploding
And having to be mopped up
Leaving bits of glitter in the mop forever

The mop leaving them on black floors
Here and there forever

Invisible Man

Just from prison
Cold bites the face

Past a dumpster, a crack in a door
Enter into warmness
Echo slam behind me like in church sanctuary

Heat coming from laundry room
Dryers and smell like childhood
Open one, find woman's coat and panties

Leave panties without smelling
Out of respect for donation of coat

They keep tumbling
No wetness tonight

Rescuing Selfishly

You are so cold
And the cold air is sucking the moisture from you

Like a mummy
Shriveled and gray
You must be resurrected
Awoken with a kiss

That will redden your lips
Filling them with blood
For me

Stung

Tingling honey from heart to ribs
Tickling and sticking

Until suddenly I taste it
As laughter bursts out of me
Like flowers

And as all the bees are secretly smiling tiny smiles
Mine is even more content than theirs

As my cheeks flush the color
Grown from the seeds of your words

Motherhood

She bears a grin of delight
With corners and visible gums
And laugh lines

No awareness of what it looks like
Only benevolence
And sunlight

Through her hair
And lining sensible clothing
As she walks up the stairs

To the door to your house
And looks at you
Telling you to come on

Even though
She doesn't know what's coming
Any more than you do

Just that more is in store
Because you're always new

Dating Ad

I don't care for most things
Can we go somewhere empty

Not even grass there
Not even shoes or coats

No candy
Just sun and colors
But not too saturated

Just tastes and lovers
But not too aftertasted

Just my temple against your forehead
And your hand in my hand

Buying Furniture

Surrounded
Textured table tops
Feeling wrong

Grain too thick or thin
Plastic in it

Not suitable
For the oils
Of men's hands upon it

Too many objects
Trinkets on shelves

Longing for not this
But can't find the sign
The exit

Discovering You

Opening a hatch to peaceful cacophony
Instead of being sucked out into space
You and your debris suck into me
Scooping me up in a swirl resembling galaxies

There is only hair and tastes and spinning
And knocking up against things I don't care to identify

Softly, with dull sounds as under water
Safely floating
In a sleeping bag attached to a wall

Amidst all the data we've accumulated
Being spat back and forth
As shiny orbs
From mind to mind

Legs intertwined
No regard for location or time

Concert Insanity

Everyone is touching
In a bed so large it's a floor
Covered in lights flashing
Vibrated all over by static guitar
Smelling and smiling

But I'm not
I'm just trying to text you
To go eat cookies and listen to blues

To not have their sweat on me
But a bath and no shoes

An Ex Moving Me Around

Clicking and dragging
And scratching his nose

And clicking
And selecting
Eyes shifting
Sighing

Short bursts of tapping
And backspacing

Clicking and dragging again
To the garbage bin
Then letting go

Magnetism

Like petals off a tree
Sliding off and into your hair

Lifting your hand to feel what they are
Surprising you by smearing softness
And scent and oil
On your fingers and your nose

Supposed to be flowers
But falling apart

Because they noticed you were below

Heat

Approach me
From the corner of the sheets
Like a creature, tiny

Let me feel you rustle them gently
Refusing to touch me

Seeing only a lump moving
Speed increasing and decreasing
Like my heartbeat

Until I pull off sheet after sheet
Seemingly infinitely

And then get into bed
With your skin and the heat within
Finally

No Subtext

There is a girl alone in bed
With a severe cramp
Between her neck and head

But not at all minding
Only because as her hair touches
Her breasts and tenderness
She notices and brushes it aside

And in the coolness of her fingertips
Feels the warmth of a kiss
Spreading soothing from neck to body

And thinks to herself
I'm not at all lonely

Longing

Let me put a seashell to your ear
Not so you can hear the sea
But so you can picture my hand near you
So you have an excuse to put your face near me

Keep listening to the ocean
And I'll lean in listening too

Even though I can't hear the ocean
Except vicariously through you

Discovering Nighttime

Lying atop a stack of magazines
I'm a shadow in a child's eye
As she searches her mom's room for anything
To make the day pass by

Reaching up at her
In the form of a face
That the brain makes from non-face matter
When the light plays with things

Zombie Lady

Falling away
Dropping everything
All of the things
I was holding
Falling out and off of me

Like a Japanese woman
Having released surrogate baby
After months of pain

Bloodied white-knuckled hands
Unclasping from splintery rope

Cord cut
No more moaning
Already standing
Walking

With sore, shaking legs
To the next thing
Eyes shining nothing

Snippets

Looking at a photo of you
In passing

While tasting my breath
And remembering
The breath of all those I've had

And knowing very certainly
That yours isn't anything like that

Trusting

Hanging upside down
Breasts dangling and everything
Just laughing and laughing

This crazy lady
At once of all ages and shapes

That you're fucking
Even though the laughs are ugly

Because you know the soul of her face

Stubborn

I'll yawn infinitely
And squirm and twist incessantly
The hips and spine popping ceaselessly

The sun will cause water to be produced from my eyes
I'll groan anciently but orgasmically
And hit the snooze button seventeen times

Coffee shops will worship me
And taxi cabs to save from lateness will line up in lines

I'll do this, all of it
I'm warning you, I'll do it

Just try and stop me

Alright, alright
Goodnight

Dog Ear Free

Yellow books on a shelf
A place for you and I to be

When the world is through with our bodies
And only our selves are left, you see

In the meantime, I'd like to taste you
Before you taste like pulp and paper

In the meantime, I'd like to face you
Before the dog ears become visible

Blatant Romantic Poem

Baby darlin'
Take me slowly
To a place of snow and ice

Take me somewhere where the wind is blowing
And kiss me
So I may experience human flight

My hands are freezin'
My toes are frozen

My clothes aren't working
I'm shivering with all my might

In hopes you'll close the door behind us
So that we may kiss tonight

Keys

A drug fiend leans half undressed over keys
Pouring out a ballad between sips of whiskey
Of days to come and future and past and all that

Falling asleep barely, with fingertips ringing notes that last
For an age, maybe an age and a half

Rope Brain

Reading up a mountain
Clutching the dots on i's
Slipping down y's
And snagging my ass on t's

Wrapping toes around o's just barely
Spreading them and reaching
Stretching out the cords in my mind

And tying them in new knots
To hold me

Sleeping Grown Up

Aching apart and flaking apart
A girl on a bed
Each part of her falling outward from her heart

Crying without crying any
Having lost the ability
As crying gland has turned to ash

And been rubbed in
With the rest of her indistinguishable pieces
Except little fingertips discernible in the dust

Monkey's Conversations

Pulling out bits of dandruff with crochet hooks
But really with fingernails that move like them
Picking bit by bit
The scalp of a friend

Finding words there
The right ones to coexist
At the right moments
And hastily eating the ones that don't

And sometimes for a second
Pulling their hair by accident
And uttering quick apology

And moving on
To keep picking
And caressing occasionally

Clean

Water trickles
Off the ends of my hair and onto your face

For you to taste it
For it to absorb in
To your tongue and your lips
Like wine does

Making you drunk instantly

Plan of Rainy Girl

A water droplet slides off paper harmlessly
And on the carpet it dissolves

And then one pools and could damage the page
And another
And another

It's too late now, I'll have to buy this book

I'm too wet from the rain to be touching printed things
But I'll repair it by covering it fully in water
In the bath later

Rationalizing Fire Sex

Fire is inefficient
It makes you smell weird

It's too hot up close
And too cold otherwise
Causing sweat on one side

Inside of crevices
Like the inner thighs
And where the knees bend

And when you go away from the fire
And unbend
The sweat gets cold

Especially if you're naked
And trying to be sexy with a fire and a man

So why do I enjoy this

Man Simulation

All the things look like a man
When a man is in your heart

You look at the bumper of a car
And it doesn't do that face bullshit
But it looks like a man saw it
And you're in his mind seeing it

And it's the same with all the stuff outdoors
Squirrels look like he's acting them as puppets
Trees are waving at you with his hands

But you're not worshipping a man
You're seeing what he might see

For a minute

Being Loved

Giggling infinitely
Like there's a tiny man stuck in my abdomen
Kissing and licking the inside of it

And because of being tiny
That tickling and being hot

And the fever of that
Infecting the rest of my body

Like a sickness made of pure blush and happiness
Heat remaining in my cheeks long after the giggling ceases

Picnic Blanket

Sunshine all up in my face
Blinding and everything
Putting rim lights on you
Between your fingers like God is coming through or something

And reflections on your eyes
Like you're smiling harder than you could possibly be doing

It's goddamn ridiculous
When every touch is like honey

Sticking to me for all time
And glowing

The sun's radiation just making me high

Having Fun

Seeing your face
Triggers a million chain reactions
Inside my brain and my hands

Until, before I know it
I'm somewhere I never could have imagined

No really, I can't
It's years later
That's how it works

Hopefully it's good
But who cares, currently
This is where your face is

Tomorrow it could be mangled or something
Into a thousand pieces

But at this moment, the worst you can do
Is stretch and twist it to imitate that

And at this moment
The worst I can do is not be able to do it back
Because of laughing too much

Blasphemy

A dinner takes place
Late at night in between life
Without candlelight
As is preferred, spontaneous

And as I search for your eyes
And cannot find them

I am destroyed as I look down to notice
The most beautiful morsel
Crafted by my improvisational hand

Crushed under your spoon
And not even looked at
Or eaten

As you get up to take back the dishes

News of Unwantedness

Obliterated under foot
Spine twisted like a dead bird on the sidewalk
And smelling like one also

The person who has fallen on the ground
In an apartment and physically unharmed
Without accident

Too Many Too Few

A lady waiting at a bus stop
Unable to be recognized as old or new

Smelling like perfumed hair after a day
Smelling like a person but awful
Smelling like something made up but picked like a flower

In a small town stretched into the space of a big city
Repeating itself
And ladies like her

Girl Training

Pin a postcard on a wall above a desk
Or stick it to a mirror

Look at yourself
Then look at it

Write a note
Then look at it

Print it with your lips
And look at their print
And wonder if the recipient sees
What you see in them

If there is a recipient
Besides the dresser clutter

Move your hips
In all directions

And wonder if an actual person
Will touch them as well as you touch them

Itchy Clothes

Pull off all of them
All of them, please
Like sticky wax paper
Stuck like cheesecloth to cheese

Peel and leave markings
Of red on my waist
Where there was elastic

Stressed by overexpansion
And wiggling

After spending an evening
Biting nails anticipating this moment
While examining your face

The Mom's Underground

The icebox light has a quality
That is like nothing else

As her robe feels its way through floor's darkness
Like a dog's snout

In a house that is empty
Except for you sleeping upstairs
She ravages in a way she wouldn't want
You to know her to be

Then, with box wine
Yawns in front of the TV
And scents of hairspray and your school day

Falls asleep peacefully
Until you are awake

Excuse House

I live inside a coffee cup
And I can't bend or curl enough

My feet are pressed against the wall
And it's round

All I can do is curl my toes
Like a cat at home alone
Waiting

Pretending to be contented
While her master is out

Eyes Open Fast

Catching breath
From a fall asleep

Down your throat
Past your teeth

Which you clench up
As you do

As you remember
That you are you

Made Up Lady

A bun in the oven
Atop her head

Deeply golden
Hole in the center
Annoying to lay on in bed

Powdered sugar
On her cheeks
Browned and rosy underneath

Tastes like minerals
And perfume and sweat
And cinnamon buns eaten

Rubbing off on the hands
And sticking on the fingers
Though not iced yet

Warm like stress

Waiting Out Sickness

Cool air through the nose and windows
Roof of the mouth like metal

Smooth and iron tasting
Swallows never stopping
Pecking at attention
Like acorns falling

Dull hurting
Throughout all of the house

Hoping it passes
Hoping the birds get bored of their pecking
Or the tree runs out

Pearl of Focus

Concentrated bubble
Pressed tighter than anything
But too slippery to squeeze

Black tapioca in the brain
Surrounded by electricity
That cannot penetrate

Aware of its existence but
Unable to touch it

A space containing everything

Lying Down

Bones cracking into the bed
Like bubble wrap stepped on slow

Oh, the satisfaction of the pops
Until forgetting that you are now deflated
And will be for at least eight hours

At least there aren't permanent holes in your bones
That you know of

Winter Workers

Stocking cap dwellers
Hovering over trashcans and stoves
Inside their own homes and workplaces

Curling into hooded sweaters
Like snails under water

Smush Worm

Rolled in the crack of a thick book
Like ash or weed or crumbs dropped
From a muffin in a coffee shop

Smeared and sprawled
My arms above my head

Breasts pressed up
And legs stretched all the way out

Face buried in the letters

Nose scrunched against the roll of the pages
And loving it like the rubbing of labia

Head Going Nuts

Cat curled up
Inside a ballerina's bun

Yowling each time
Her twirls are spun

And scratching each time
She tries to get it undone

Delicacy

One at a time peas
On fork tips

Lined up in a row all squeezed
Squishy round from a can
Alien orbs like painted by hand

Being poor not a sign of destruction
But a shade of green

Wishing for Sustenance

Eating through your heart
Chewing it up like red velvet
Then coughing it up like a cat with grass

Gnawing on good tasting garbage
Then turning it to vomit on the carpet

Wishing that instead it would sink in and digest
And feeling sad because of that

Convertible Hair

Tell me where we're going
I don't want to know
But tell me
So I can see your lips moving

As we drive to and fro
The wind is blowing
And we're catching the sun

Who cares where we're going
Our last day alive has begun

Concave Town

Cobblestones twisting ankles
Whether you run or you walk
It always feels angled

Streets a million feet all
Climb up them
With these foot holds
Under your palms

Then walk barefoot into the ocean
And forget where you are

And that water could pour into it
Like a submerging bowl

Night Music Car

Riding the wave of sound
In a car on the ground

Feeling the wheels roll over you
As you're above them

LIke the wheels of a toy car
As your child pretends your leg is a mountain

Getting Away

Vacation to the bedroom
And to the kitchen too

Avoiding all the restaurants
And all the hotel rooms
That do not offer the taste of you

Good Hair Day

Parting the hair like a sea
With waves rolling up like curls of ink

Dandruff surfers riding them
Catching the breeze

Made With Love

Between my palms is a squishy clay
Rubbing its self all over me
As I rub myself into its shape

Hiding it under my handprints
Like a lightning bug that might escape

Afraid to look at the hardening
Beautiful thing I've created

Out of Breath

Running through a crowded street while walking
And yelling your name without saying a word

Not looking like me at all but looking like light
Shining through all the people to your table
That you were sitting at alone until you felt the glow

And you picking me up by looking at me
And spinning me around by standing facing me

And knowing that you might touch my hand

Outside

Trying another day
Another time of tying shoes
Another vitamin to take
Another glass of orange juice

And crossing of streets
And light from the sky
Tingling the eyes
Reflecting in them blue

And wind with smells in it
And trying on voices and laughs

And people-watching
And telling them to you

Beautiful Entanglement

Big orange coat of flowers
Smelling so much that it's on when it's not

A whole bunch of flowers woven together
By some child playing pranks while you sleep in the grass

Beautiful and woven like braids on the head
But itchy and tight like a net
Holding you down to the earth

As though they grew through you
Like through a grave
Through the dead

Paparazzi Sand

I can't see anything
I'm buried in sand

It's as though just one tiny grain
Is very close up
And has blacked out my vision

And all the other grains
Are lined up behind it

And the ones that couldn't fit in the line
Are crowded around them

Waiting their turn
Wishing to speak to me
And get an autograph

Looney Toons

Peanut butter and saltine crackers
Falling crumbs on the counter

Light is dim and not from this kitchen
But from the den where the cartoons are

As we pause to get our refreshments
And reenter over soft barefoot carpet

As the theme song starts

Wet Hair

A cool rain in a drought
Falling down
In streams heavy

Erasing the scents of yesterday
And the scraggly grass

Ending the great depression
For a moment
And leaving dew

For the morning sunlight to touch

Filled With Water

Not sure whether love is real
A touch on the head felt so long ago

Floating happily in a sun-drenched boat
Not really worried about the shore

I've been moving and bobbing for so long
The sloshing and my insides are one

I can't get sea sick anymore
And I've fished and fished and made this my own

It seems I might suffocate if I touch sand
It seems that if I touch dry land I'll fall over

And collapse
Spilling out all over

False Tattoo Identity

Dropping a pen on a leg
Dotting it with a freckle

Feeling drawn
Rather than clumsy
For a moment

Wanting to be a starry sky forever
And the next day

Covering every natural freckle
Making a terrible mistake

Growing Into Body

Moving like a woman
But feeling like a man

Crouching in shame of this
Spine curving and hair covering head

Hands tentative
Arms too narrow to lift
Legs impossible to hide

Sticking out long like the pole of a flag
A baggy shirt that flaps in the wind

Blowing taut occasionally
Revealing in a moment of no self-consciousness
The contour of breasts

Bittersweet

Chocolate swirling into all places
Into every wrinkle as though you're an elephant

Drying up and making you delectable
A mix of sweat and sweetness and depression

So much sadness has caused so much chocolate
To coat you all the way through

But even with all this chocolate
The tears will happen
And leave lines all over you

Reminding what your real, soft skin was
Before you took on this transcendent form
Of mud and goo

Teenage Moment

Inside my freckle is a whole world
Only known about by you and me

Or at least that's what it seems like right now
As I stare at my arm

And you stare at my arm
To share an interest with me

Thinking About Typing

Hand outstretched and floating
In the diffused light of the white screen

Dainty or contorting
Or imitating mannerisms seen

It can be anything
But best not to look at it

Best to look at the screen

Drunk Alone in Dark

Falling on the floor
From walking on pants legs not on all the way

Glad that no one is aware or can see

Maybe someone below heard the thud
But they have no way of proving why it happened

Even if they imagine why it happened
Or you tell them during nervousness later

It's not on your permanent record
Like driving would be

Claimed Suddenly

Big hands on the throat
Warmth and heat like a fire and a coat

Not even having to be pressing
Moving down the body slow

Making you aware of its presence
Freezing you like the cold of a ghost

Upholstery Nap

Snuggling into the car
The backseat like a sleeping bag
With the smell of trips
And sleeping happening scrunched

Face pressed into seat back
But not too bad
Because it is a nineties car
The square kind with a couch as a back

And you are here
Curling my hair around my ear

While I pretend to be asleep and not notice

Pinky Swear

Don't forget the way our fingers are touching now
Even when you have lost all these cells
And your fingers are entirely new ones

And your nerves are slightly different
And you've felt other fingers

Screen Door

He's gone and the wind blows
The dust past my front door

And hair suffocates my nose
Like a ghost for a sec

And then my eyes are wet as I cough
And when they focus, still he's gone

Sunrise Sunset

My big blanket is good and big
The yellowness of it is pale
Like the sun on the edge of Mom's hands
And on the windowsill

And now I will leave this bed
And we will walk to look at potted plants and plant them
And I will sip cappuccino and Italian ices with a fresh haircut

And carry the water bottle that glistens as we walk back
With bellies full of McDonalds and movies
And cramps from walking full of all this and not minding that

And then by the fireplace we'll rest
My head on her chest
Staving off the bitterness of the sunset on our walking

Embracing our bodies becoming softness
And entering the mode of TV marathoning

Summer at its end

Frozen Spaghetti Moment

All the kisses are so good
Above and below

And all the flavors are so good
From your brow to your toes

And I want your legs to wrap me up forever
And mine to wrap up yours
And my waist in your arms

Around a beautiful fork together
Never all the way slurped up

Heavy Chest

Cat's tail curled around my throat
Claws deep in my chest with love
Fur breathed in my nose

All this, a note that says
If you leave me you're dead
Don't go

Animal Blood

Eat me in the bed
Eat me up whole

Be like a lion that I'm climbing in
Eyes old with knowingness
Tongue warm and teeth thick

And my skin unable to be penetrated
Made for this moment and impervious

My legs around your throat like cobras
Squeezing you merciless

Moving around your blood
And stimulating it

Prophetic Fever

Here on the dining room floor
I can see my family's future

Their names are coming out of my mouth
Mom says it's the fever

But it's that I know what's gonna happen
To everybody
And it's all really bad

And it's making me realize strongly
How good it is being ten

But I know I'll forget all of it
Once I'm put to bed

Pile of Building

Filth in numbers
Pouring out of bathrooms
And kitchens and floors

Whole floors of dust and cat hair
And women laying down in unmade beds

With stuff under their fingernails
Smoke in their lungs
And worries in their heads

And two or three of us
Buried amongst all this

Sipping something hot
And tapping away at tasks

Youthful Age

Tired always
Days spent exerting excitement

Throat like a child's that has screamed
With ears covered

Leap

Water in the brain straight-up
Like cocaine

Wondering whether for a second it's really a thing
The speediness I'm up to with no caffeine

Hopefully no crash will occur
I'm assuming
So long as I remain sane

And slow down nightly
To make love in the rain

Even though I'm making love constantly
At this point

Eyes

Who was the first person
Who told another person to close their eyes

Was it for calming or for hiding
Or for listening or for sex
Or for death in disguise

Did it confuse the person
To think about being asleep or being dead
As something to be done awake and alive

And when they found it pleasant
Were they surprised

Or had they been doing it on their own for ages
And when someone told them to, they said
No, these eyes are mine

Landfill

Days uncompleted
Left in piles of clothes here and there on the floor

Meant to be put back on
After a nap
That lasts a whole season

Waking up with them out of style
And in between making them
Hours build up to denouements

That never happen except in spirit
Once all the resources and all the clean laundry
Are depleted and gone

Infinite Women

Malignant apartments
Sprawling time and space

With women inside them
Cooking chickens and putting makeup on their faces
Not in that order maybe
But something like that

That's the thing is no matter how many of them
No matter how many of us
We can't make up our minds on the order of things

And we can't stand that we don't
Know how long we'll live

Statue

When you lift me, I feel like a ballerina
High above your head

When all you're doing is placing your hands on
My ribs below my breasts

And stroking me softly
So it feels like music

While your eyes search my face
For all the signs that you're making me happy

That my mind is spinning
That your hands have found their place

Next Room Over

Guitar strums can be heard
And sometimes vibrations and sighs

Sometimes crazy laughter
And silly voices
Talking to herself for a long time

Sometimes outbursts of crying
Followed by whimpers very soft

Sometimes pots and pans clanking
Dishes done at four o'clock

So much sound in early morning
And very late at night

Except for music in the daytime
Then slamming doors
To be gone for a while

Warmth

We have loved infinite

A kiss on the forehead
Hair pressed into your cheek's skin

Scents of having been in
And held in a blanket
All these cold winters
Lived in this moment

A sweater just gotten
Already having been worn
Again and again

And the warmth of it inside us
Never having left
From other lives we've spent

Sticking

Your legs stick to this wooden chair
When it's cold and when it's not
It doesn't matter, skin just does that

That's why it's important if I were to paint you
To indicate the sticking going on

Artists always talk about shadows
From things making contact

But they don't talk about sticking
Unless they're talking about movement

But sticking is all over
And sticking hurts when it's ripped off
Creating red marks

And I'd like to stick to you for now
So you can be convinced of how much

An Uncomfortable Night

Home in a stomachache

Brought back to ten years old
By merely having to sleep
Without having ate

And being cold
Although covered in sheets and blankets
That are tucked under the mattress
And taut

Feeling a guest
In my own home

A child staying here for the night

Couch Jokings

I could cry from how much I love you, you know
Even when laughing the hardest

And even when covered in this blanket
That covers the legs of the both of us

Although it covers just my two
And yours are somewhere else

I cover mine for yours as well
I reserve the extra warmth

Anticipating Fingertips

Light and sugar
Dripping off your hands

Not sticky at all
But like water
But sweet like kisses

All the tingling that will happen
When those beauties touch my skin

Makes it so there's nothing else
But waiting for them

Checking In

Sometimes when I lay here
And you touch my thigh

Or well, I mean
When my hand is on it
And I can feel your hand through mine

I can feel you checking on me
In ways I wouldn't check myself

There's no reason for me to squeeze
The way you squeeze me

There's no reason for me to feel this caressed
When touching myself

Stepping Out

Outside laying on the ground
Getting covered in leaves

Then covered in snow
Then in grass
Peeking up through your skin

That breeze
Then dry
Then cold
Then tingle wet

All that in this moment of stepping out

Of foot hitting cement
After being in and dead forever

Upside Down

Sometimes you have to hang upside down on the bed
And look at the whole room
And appreciate its put-togetherness
And complexness that you forgot
From being in it so long

You'll see the colors and textures more
You'll see how pink stands out
And is peppered everywhere
And how light makes dark wood shine

Like when painting a picture
And turning it upside down
To refresh your eyes

Skinny Fat

A girl gets fat and doesn't even know it
She's never been fat before, so how would she know

Things just seem smaller
Buttons are harder to push
She just figures that somehow
She's continued to grow

She was always thin
Proportions were always off back then

She just figures that somehow
She's finally catching up

She just figures that somehow
She's finally grown up

Thighs are fuller than before
And it's fun to grab them
The roundness is enjoyable

She just figures that finally
Her breasts are big enough

She just figures that finally
She'll be fun to touch

Comic Book Hair

Hair becomes soft and smooth on its own
It helps to not have a cat for a while
So you can just pet sections of it
Over and over

If you let it grow and do this
And wash and condition it every so often
And comb it a couple times a day, of course

You really won't ever need a straightener
Or a curler
Or even a brush

It'll just do pleasant stuff
On its own
That you don't expect

Cartoon stuff
Comic book hair
As you get older

And it happens like this
With other stuff too

You just get used to your superpowers
Pretty much

Multiple Deaths Alone

Sometimes you don't even know how to cry anymore
And just feel like sleeping

But don't know how to sleep anymore
So you just sit awake thinking of nothing

Except maybe that you're supposed to be
Feeling something more

And then eventually you get up
And do everything
And it hurts like fuck

But after it's over
Every hug feels like a nap in the sun

Or like falling asleep on each other
With the TV on

Hopeful Sweater

Wearing my reddest shirt today
All about the sweater fuzz

Makes dimples stand out when I smile
Or at least I like to think

It's a date shirt
Like someone would wear in a movie maybe

Whether he's present or isn't
It's good to look ready
For a date

Short Girl Glamour

Sometimes I wish I was a short girl
That could be picked up and raised up high
And rolled around and kissed leaning down

With a waist like a handle and tiny, fat thighs
And little high heels like in the displays
That come in each and every type

And every man tall and every man brave
Holding my little hand and holding me tight

Air Approaching

Alone in the darkness
On Christmas Eve night

The air feels like stillness
And radiator scents

Hair feels like moistness
Ears are squeaky and fresh

Little sounds of grinding
Of feet and pipes
And keys late getting in

And cabinets shutting and opening quiet
As though the person on the other side
Is more considerate than expected

It seems as though there's things reminding me
Everywhere I look and sniff
To choose rightness in the moment

And treat air like cookie icing
Instead of like coldness
Remaining stiff

You Wake Me Up

When my knees are pulled to my chest
At my desk late at night

And the words you've written
Let out from your heart
Are given generously as gifts to my eyes

My mouth on my knee feels like kisses
My weariness is forgotten
My skin remembers warmness
Other than mine

And then I go to sleepiness
Which feels the opposite
Of what's really in my mind

Screen in Dark

Light me in the darkness
Dark now's not so bad
Dark now is highlights on wood
That I can feel with my hand

Wood is comforting
When it's smooth
And matches other wood

When it's wood of one's own choosing
In a space that's dark and full of no one

Except for me and the minds I'm learning
All these parts of me coming back one by one

In words they wrote to find me
When they were alone in the dark

Blank TV 2002 - 2016

Television in front of me and I wish you'd come out of it
I see myself and I want to see you
I wish you'd come out of it and kiss me and eat me alive

I watched a movie once that I was terrified of
I was folding laundry alone when I was twelve
I wound up sitting in the laundry basket alone
Mere feet from the screen that spelled my death

From there on I saw her everywhere
I'd see myself and I'd see her
For years to come in shadows and corners

And now that I'm free of her finally
And don't fear being alone

I kind of miss her
And want someone like her in a lover

Brushing Your Face

Brown and only brown
I want your vision to be
Just brown for a little while
Until I decide to leave

You won't mind, I promise
You'll forget the other colors exist

Then when I finally lift my hair
From your forehead

It'll be like you're gifted the world again

Your Own Love

He's in the wind
When the little birds come
And cast a shadow on the walls like in a film
And no one notices except I do

Love sort of has to be that way
God sort of has to be your own

No matter how many people look up at the sky
No one feels the same thing
No one thinks the same thing

As a Man

I wish I were a man
I wish I could cum in a woman
And give life
And go away on my own

To explore other women
And other places
And not even ever be found

To not have to wait
Nine months gestation
To put a child into the world

I could just cum and cum
And run and run

And leave my influence
Fast enough that I have no death
And no stagnation anymore

No People

Train sounds and moon shines
Through the window late at night

Out there are
Flat, wide grounds and open skies
Diagonal roads
Colored doors placed behind

Empty cars and darkened signs
Off light poles and power lines

Black silhouettes blending as one
Moonlight on backdrops
Buildings sitting as though hung

Sometimes a light will come on
Then after a little go off
In a way automatic
No people to be found

A feeling of being watched
By the very air

Teenage Suburb Cam

Remember when we used to edit
With dark circles under our eyes
From smeared eyeliner
From the day
And hair a mess
No lipstick on

Remember when we used to run
Along the creeks in Converse shoes
And step in puddles and leave the footprints
On the cement between the walls

Remember when we used to come up with
Greater ways to make fools of ourselves
Things to smash and things to draw on
And a camera like any old tool
If we dropped it and had to get a new one
That was ok

Bear Arms

Big arms that aren't
That aren't there at all
But God am I wrapped up
With warm caressing love

Being held hard
So tight that it blends in
To my body like lotion
But better than that

Coating me like a big fur coat
In the Arctic

Made out of a bear with the sharpest claws
But only using them for clamping
And hurting more to let go

Cartoon Man and I

Cartoon man
Perfectly everything I ever wanted
And me perfectly everything I want to be
When around him

And there are big smiles on our faces
Our cheeks are prominent and we like to touch them
Against each other and lock eyes beaming

And hold each other like nothing is more precious
And just stay like that doing nothing else
But being delighted in each other's existence

Piano Wood

Piano wood lingers here
Dust made out of it
And younger versions of us

Its scent is like the slam that happens
If you close the door
Above the keys too fast

Sunset Market

I'm the only person around
I got off the bus
As the sun goes down
It's still going down
And I gotta decide which way to walk

I'm not usually in the market
When it's empty

There are no trucks
And the stores are chained up

There's only me and the yellow
On the edges of the metal and the bricks

And the air and the warmth
And the ground is flat and wide and long
And I like that there's no one

I like that I chose to ride this far
And get off here
For no reason

Maybe I will do the same again
But farther, to the river next time
To see the sun set on it and the train bridge

Wrapped Around You

Red blanket waves are rolling
Their brushing sounds like water spray
Crashing on shores with sunsets on them
All over the world

All over my legs
Which are all over you

Rubbing up and down you
Forever and ever
Wherever you sleep

Drowning High

I love you in the water
Far away in outer space
Where there aren't others
And hair floats
And frames our face

I cannot breathe here
But I look like I'm breathing so much

As my body's swelling and swelling
As my eyes start to leave my mind

Just Flowers

When I was four
And all alone up in my room
Flowers weren't a thing of death
Or a thing of love

They were made of paper
And purses made out of them too

And in ribbon trims on dresses
In the middle of little bows

Alone here just doting on them
Unaware of their role

And outside, just picking them
Unaware they took work to grow

Zipper

A seam in a friend
Ready to be unzipped
But sometimes jammed

Up and down
Jerking it
Crying a little
In frustration

Knowing they're too hot
Knowing they love you

Even though their zipper
Hurt your hand

Flower Love

Flowers on me because you put them there
Otherwise naked
And naked anyway

Flowers are like part of me now
Their petals are mine
And mine are theirs

The scents blend together
The oils blend together

What did I look like before flowers
Before your kisses sprang up
And made them grow

I must have been a big old dust bowl
A great depression without my love

Teenage Foreplay

A new piece of France
Was invaded today

Fingers entered a girl
With brown eyes and French braid

And frenching was done
And a bra was opened up

And an avalanche rolled out
Whole mountains fell
Atop his American cock

But in the end
No red, white and blue
Only blue balls

And a lonely bedroom
With slammed echoing door

With French textbook
And panties hidden
Somewhere on the floor

With her gone quick
And Mom's TV on out there

Man Girls

Little scrawny worrywarts
With shoulders up to their cheekbones
Their bare bodies are always uncomfortable
Pants don't know how to sit on them

Talk is always nervous
Like something about to be found out
Or someone just got caught

Angriness comes out unexpected
To intimidate those who listen well

The eyes are scared of being noticed
The voice begs for it like a child
Always asking a question

The posture runs away without them
All while standing up in a tall slouch

A mess of body parts gone different directions
All standing in a pile

Dinner Table

Holding hands across a table
Across all the tables
In all the restaurants
From here to there

Feet pressed next to each other
Under a table
And every table
From here to there

Next to broken glass on floors
And next to seeing eye dogs
Of old women in wheelchairs
And next to bits of food dropped

Eyes looking past it all
At each other
Across the table

And smiles so subtle
But so unmistakable

That I can feel it in my heart
And no food is needed

Edge of Bed

Trapped in a bed till morning
Only leaning off is allowed

Sometimes leaning all the way
Until only the feet touch
In a big, long pushup
On one hand
To grab a toy

Children are dextrous
When you tell them no

When you give them limits
To play with and walk on

Awaiting Your Cooking

Just your cooking
Your cooking alone

Just your cooking
You're cooking a love

Just keep looking
Looking across
Across the room behind your back

Your smells are words
Finger-painted
On my heart with sauce

In my mouth with smiles
Happening invisible
From your front

Airport Smooches

Airport smooches
In the middle of the night

Suddenly appearing
Out of thin air
Surrounding me and shining

A tingly new place for now

Then gone again
Back to sleep in these waiting room chairs

Back to neck cramps
Remembering neck kisses

That nobody saw
Not sure if it was real or not

First Sight

There is a crowd pulling hard
I can see your eyes and mouth

And the twitch of your cheek
That means movements inside
Of tears that form in the muscles alone

For some reason I'm being taken off
Before our hands can reach or touch

And we have never seen each other before
Or heard each other's names
Or heard us talk

Until finally here and we could rip apart
All these people and every column

Just to stop us being swept up
Out of this moment we need so much

Hug During News

A hug in the dark
Where no one can see us

Only to feel
And feel and feel

Tears on your shoulder
And nothing in between us

Warm in a building
Saying nothing

With the sound of the news

Tall Girl Wishes

I'm too big and tall
My ankles are thick like trees

My arms are long
My hands are as big as yours

But my heart fits in your palm
My soul is cradled
In your arms like a child

I have the figure of a short blonde
And the voice of an angel
Because my love for you
Makes me glow like gold

So let's eat food
And look into our eyes like glows
Of our sweet cores
Beyond the visuals we hate of ourselves

And that's all you look like when I look
And I look like a girl
In your heart

Not a basketball star

Droplets

My breast milk is growing
Droplet by droplet
It's storing itself up

Everything is helping it
Like carrots and chocolate

And kind words soft spoken
And each one of your kisses
On skin so soft

One day I'll have filled them
If I eat enough

And we fuck enough
And I enjoy enough sun

One day a first drop will come out
Beginning of many droplets in life
For a whole human

Roller Coaster

So close yet so far
Man between my legs and in my heart

My voice echoes sounds of yours
Inside of mine
Tickling me hard

I cannot sing
But you pull my sweetness out

I have no grace
But you make me float

I can feel your fingers
All down my sides
Falling like a roller coaster
So good I could cry

And it must be a water one
Coming out of me

When it gets to the bottom
Of my belly

I Dig You

Running through the city
Where no one knows no one

And may as well be buried and gone
Peoples from some time to figure out

I look like I've been on a dig
And I found you

I'm makeupless and in clothes
That fit like my soul does
Jeans and cotton and tennis shoes

And hair that's tossed perfect
By accident
I may as well be clothesless

You've been running as hard as you could
For hours and years and months

And now, with the dirt on our souls and our soles
And on our feet bottoms and our bottoms
And under our nails and in the air around us

We look like we're shining anyhow
In soft light and music
Embracing like a movie scene, delighted

Two people alive
Digging each other up
And washing the dirt with kisses

Becoming Food

Folded up hips
Protruding real soft
The little bit of fat
That happens when scrunched

Even when you're thin
And clean and tall
If you fold into a ball
While perched atop a chair
With no clothes at all

You'll soon have round
And squeezable parts

And feel like a sweet sticky cinnamon roll
And someone might want
To eat out your heart

Right Now Window

Cars have gotten different, haven't they
Since I woke up
Since the time when I lost my mind
And came back just now

People walk differently
Or do they walk the same
As they did when I was a little child

There was just a time
When I wasn't equipped to notice them
In between then and now

Trees look inside of paintings
And related to the clouds
Which remind me of flying in airplanes

And so do the sounds around me
Which remind me of traveling in general
To places besides this one

I do not have to be anywhere specific
To feel what is around
I just have to be in it
And allow the present to happen

A view from a window
Is a view from a window
If the view is good

(Cont.)

Whether you're in Paris
Or Kansas City
You can see a flock of birds

And if your love were there with you
He'd comment on the pedestrians
As you do in your thoughts

Is This It

Heartbreak in the form of nothingness
Having all material things wanted
Having presence of ones loved
But no climax

No deep stares in the eyes moments
No tiny, careful kisses
No hard ones

Just lots of touching no one
Like being with your parents
But never knowing them

Love Glow

I like my hand
On wood
With the light on
With the air on

Light on the tips of all
Like gold

Licking everything with my fingertips
With my eyeballs
With my ear holes

Feeling held
Your hands on my soul

Musical presence
Lighting up the room

Tingling and smiling
A physical feeling of love

Furnace

Give me a kiss
So long that snow piles
On top of our heads
And our shoulders
And the toes of our boots
But we don't feel it

Our bodies are the outside of our house
We feel warm in our mouths
And forever fed

And between where our hearts are
Is a furnace that we insulate well

Love Overflow

All full of love
Pouring out my nose all gross

Snot-like and wiping up with napkins
Cocktail napkins in a bar
And people staring and holding back laughter

And coming out my eyes as tears
With joy and smiles

Sticking my tongue out at the people
Because who cares

It can keep coming out of it wants
It'll never dry up
All this love I have

Past Mopes

I never liked my family
I never wanted them all

But when they were gone I was weeping
Being mistreated by boys
Doing nothing and showing it off

Soup makes a ring in a near empty bowl
In my lap in my home

Where no one goes and no one cleans
And people go less when I don't clean

Which is often to keep them off
Somewhere else where I'm not

Who are people
I don't know what they are

What is getting up
Before noon

What are curtains
What's it like having a dog

Baggage

Holding on to hell
Heavy heart and twisted nails

Hanging up like upside down
But self-imposed
Like acted frown

Carrying the dusty road
You've walked on daily
From child to old

Rolled up on your back
Like a sleeping bag
For staying awake

Sleeping Dog Man

Green grass pillows
Hills under your elbows

How big they are, I don't know
How big you are, I don't know

Your head rests on blades
And they look so massive
From your perspective

All else is vast blur
But you could be huge
From its perspective

You could be God
To that girl over there
Doing yoga while you're resting

Seeing nothing far away
And smelling grass
And feeling air

Rope Burn Lover

My lover and my friend
I love so much
Weaving in and out of me
Like a bunch of kissing knots

Tickling and squeezing
With every word and touch
You know what's up my alley
You're in it so much

I will never untangle
I'm tied in a knot
And I like to wriggle
Within your hold

I like to make you tighter
And see my skin turn red

I like to feel your love
I like to feel it burn

Confused and Excited

So much energy in my chest
That sleeping is tough
And all is abuzz

I want to do it all
In this moment

I want to live ninety years
Right now

All the air feels like an ocean
Big and beautiful as hell
And filling my lungs

My eyes are wide and I'm coughing
But I'm ok once I wake up

I'm alive and I'm safe once I wake up
Am I awake

It's time to wake up

Hurry Up, Be Cured

Weird dreams of wasted days
Inside of them
Inside the same

Starting over again
Tomorrow is another
Able to not be this way
Oh please no more this way

Let's not behave unbecoming as such
That all the things around
Should wither and be dead
Because of my witheredness
Because of my hanging head

And for what I don't know
It's not that I'm a zombie
Who has to live in a shadow
That isn't what I am
I've escaped that

For what reason then
Do I move so slow like this
And eat like a loris
And drop a glass

Is it stuck in me
This fearful emptiness
Will it ever leave me
Can it be gone

Dead

Unable to do anything but lay
Like a man in jeans and torn tee
Smoking a cigarette before sleep
After work that doesn't pay

After making messes
And cleaning up fewer each day

Eating nothing
But what can be microwaved
On paper plate

Ash under fingernails
Fingers calloused yellow and gray

Smelling like leather every day
Whether it's from jacket or from sweat

Or from some kind of death seeping
Through the skin

Real Care

Do you ever cross your eyes
To get that feeling
Like you're going on a roller coaster

It feels weird
But feels good

I forget to unless I'm high as fuck
Not in a manner from a drug
But in the way where the tongue sticks out
Because you don't have a care in the world

About headaches or tomorrow or life or now
Or even such things as real roller coasters

Riding those things and those chemicals
Are necessary when you're so numb that it hurts

But when you remember how to feel love
And to fall hard to the ground
And to be risen up
Shot up to the sky
And down with hurt

Nothing is necessary besides that ride
Of the real right now
Of real care

Your Love and the Sun

Babe
I haven't felt forever
With anybody
I haven't felt forever alone

I feel five years old with everybody
And contrary to popular belief
That's not good

But with you
I feel old
As the sun

And with you
I feel warm
As the cat that lies under it

And nobody can tell me
Where or when life goes

Because I know
Until it explodes
There'll always be your love
And the sun

Your Set

Put on your pants
In a room with lamps all around
And a TV and a couch

And one of those hangers for coats
And curtains on the windows
And lights that twinkle outside

It's dimly lit
And you're in love

Pick up your keys and go out
Lock the door

And bring with you your heart
Bring with you your spot
That no one else knows

But is ready to hold your love
Ready to hold
Whatever it is you will find

Because the longer you live
In a home that looks like a show

The more you'll believe it in your mind

Endless Money

Don't need that much
To be happy

Though it's taken a while
It hasn't taken a lot

Don't need every outfit I bought
Don't need to be famous

Or to sail to the moon
For if I've got you
I'm high

Just give me your voice
With your hands over my eyes

Coming up from behind
And saying
I've got you

Just give me your smile
When I turn around

And I'll feel like
I have endless money

Soaked

I need you like water
Even more so

I forget to drink water
But you I cannot

I need to swim in you
I need you covering my body
And filling my pores and holes

I need you in my eyeballs
And in my lungs
And between my toes

I need you in my blood
Where oxygen goes

Kissing my body
Every molecule

Man and World

Sleepy loved one
Safe from harm

In a bedroom
In a borough
With a computer
In a lap

Eyes starting to droop
Drifting off
As am I

Waiting patiently
For this message
And now it's here

It says
Goodnight love

Goodnight man
Reading this before all

Goodnight reading person
Stop reading now

Put your bookmark in
Let your eyes close

(Cont.)

All is right
With this world

Open me again tomorrow
If you want to

Man and world
Tomorrow

Old Together Now

Let's travel together
And do lots of puzzles
And read lots of books
When we're home

Let's discuss the newspaper
And do the crossword
And laugh at the funnies
As a couple

Let's eat a big breakfast
And wake up early
And go to bed at a decent hour

Let's dress nice
And walk like we're not in a hurry
And smile and observe
And enjoy our time

(Cont.)

Let's be old
Together now
For oldness is not promised
And is already inside

That way if we grow old together
It's just a bonus
On top of our life

Perfume

The perfume of Judy
Is very special
I remember so well
But have almost forgot

I wish I hadn't forgot
While she was near me
I didn't realize
Until I knew no one
That I knew her so well

People didn't know
How she looked in her nightgown
Or what it was to sleep
In her turquoise bed
With cold feet touching all night

(Cont.)

And then in the morning
To see her head with a towel
Silhouetted in the bathroom light

People didn't know
What her fingernails washing
My hair in the kitchen sink felt like

People didn't know the smell of the baths she ran for me
Or about the reflection I saw in the doorknob

They didn't have the hot lemon pudding
That was left over when we made meringue pie

Perfect Love Girl

She's in a space that's special to you
All alone yet connected to all

She's on your bed in your heart
And all your veins are pumping blood

And as you breathe she glows brighter with your love
And if you feel suffocated, her color dulls

You want so badly to touch her
But she is so very small

(Cont.)

You would have to tear your own heart apart
Killing her as well
To feel her skin so soft

But she is in your soul

Unhappy Ending

Candle wick smoke
Filling your lungs
From a thousand candles blown out at once

An evening ended
A thousand times
When she says
No you may not
No we may not

You used to love this smell
In small doses

Even though they make devices
To stop the smoke
When putting the candle out
You ignored them
Ever since you were a child

But now you will buy them
Several, in case you lose the first
Because you never again can be reminded
Of how you didn't fall asleep with her

Hard To Sleep

It's hard to sleep when you are feeling
That everything is calling your name

When it's love you're craving
And you're getting it
Finally

It's hard to sleep when you could wake up
And have missed everything
Like so many times you have

You'd rather stay up till you fall asleep by accident
Hopefully in the arms of the one you love by then

Love Hate

I hate my city
I don't want you to know anyone I know

I'll come there
And I'll bring it with me
All the good parts
That I love so much
And leave the bad

If you love me, you'll love them
And leave the rest alone

You will never have to see
How immensely boring

Or how rude
Or how cruel
Or how poor or how rich

You'll never have to see the ugly buildings

Only the antique houses
And the libraries
And the museums

London Fog

Gimme some fog in a cup of tea
Foaming the top
A swirling galaxy

Let me be tiny
A little person on just one of the bubbles
On the lip of my cup
As I come rushing towards me

Let me see all my troubles
Pouring down my throat

Heavy syrup of sadness
Relief, pleasure and warmth
Hot soothing life speaking to my soul

Chased with air-touched light
In the form of froth

Worries turned cold because they're dead now
Emitting bittersweet aftertaste
Of bergamot

Laugh and Fuck

Make me laugh while we fuck
Make me smile while I cum

Make our faces blush
Laugh too hard to talk

Make my whole body tickle
While I shake on your cock
And fall over on you

And make the neighbors wonder
What kind of people we are

I just love you so much

Beautiful Hat

Being in love is like a beautiful hat
That you can't describe
And have never seen anywhere
But suits you more than anything else

And even though no one can see it
You wear it everywhere

And you smile because you know it's beautiful
Complimenting all your features

Making your cheeks perk up with dimples
Making your eyes widen
Making your teeth shine through your lips

You feel like you look kissable
Although you normally don't find yourself appealing

But now you feel invincible

As long as you have your hat on
You're good
You can do anything

Magic Liquid

I want to create my own magic liquid
And soak myself in it
And come out naked

Covered in sauce of my own design
That tastes so good you want to drink it
As your eyes roll back in your head in delight

And drinking it will make you feel better
And look better from inside out

And everyone will want to buy it
But it won't work unless you make it yourself

Sweet and Salty

I'm gonna smooch you
I'm gonna fill you up with my love
So that you'll never be hungry
Except for food that we enjoy

And still you'll have sorrow
But only the necessary kind

The good kind that feels good in your soul
Like when a part of a movie makes you cry

And when it happens
I'll smooch you with sugar
On the salty tears beneath your eyes

Then we'll smooch each other
Tasting sweet and salty goodness
And our hearts will be just fine

Sober

I'm old but I'm young
All the things you put off
I'm doing right now

Giving my body
The love it wants

When you're old you will wish
You'd taken your vitamins
Instead of just
Getting drunk on the lawn

When you're old you will wish
You'd had some young cock
The kind that belongs
To a man who is old
But is also young

That smiles in a way
That resembles the sun
On the edges of a cold glass of water
Dripping with sweat

And not in a way
Like a man with raised up collar
Outside a bar
WIth a cigarette and a phone

Smells of Childhood

Boiled chicken
Wet cat food
Sardines
Tuna
Cat litter box

Candle burnt out
Perfume that's too potent
Cigarette smoke

Laundry detergent
Murphy's Oil soap
Lead paint and dust
Old wood and marble

Grass and marijuana
Rain puddles
Dirt on knees and earthworms

Hairspray and mousse
Overused hairbrush

Clothes from the store
Clothes that were not washed

Bread in the oven
Halloween fake blood
VHS plastic

(Cont.)

Morning breath
Mom's sleep musk

Grandma's perfume
Eggs cooking when waking up

Nothing and Something

This candle smells like nothing
And this room smells like nothing

Maybe that is good
Because it is clean

Something is missing though

I'd like to smell something
Besides myself
And the food I cook

And the dishes that are dirty
And the soap
Then nothing once more

But what

I will not know
Until I smell something

Far from here
Familiar but unknown

Splinter

There is a cringe in my heart
For several people
Who I love but despise
Who I feel for

Who remind me of myself
In parts

Parts that are like a splinter
That cries and cries painful

Ignoring it is impossible
But so is getting it out
So I work with it

And eventually
It works itself out
And falls on the ground

And when it's gone
When the pain is gone

I can't help but feel for a while
That I have lost a part of myself

Wilting Fabric

It's time for coats soon
It's time to retreat into one's self
Even when outside

The urge to cross arms is growing
The need to press legs together
And to rub them tight

The need to put hands in pockets
And pull collars and hoods and hats
Over the ears

And dig the chin and nose
Into a scarf or sweater
To warm with breath

Fogging glasses
And lots of lotion
For cracking hands

Will this all
Make me look better or worse

Will I be buried
Or exaggerated
As the layers thicken my frame
And my face pops out amongst them

Like a flower in a wasteland
The only bit of flesh that exists

Ornament

There's a real you and there's a real me

I have to buy your family presents
Because they're real
And part of you
So they're part of me

I have to decorate the tree on Christmas
And make sure that we have enough to eat

It's no longer just me in my apartment
It's you and me and everyone we touch
And shared air we breathe

And I'm so lucky I get to hold it
And feel the cold and the heat
When all I had was popcorn and string

And I hope to God I don't drop it
Like the most beautiful shiny
Delicate ornament

Not just a graphic
On a screen

Perpetual Symptoms

Perpetual chest ache
But not from sickness

Perpetual tingling
But not being tickled

Perpetual walking on air
But not trained in ballet

Perpetual salivating
But not conditioned

Perpetual tears
But not feeling sad

Perpetual sore pussy
Definitely from your bed

Symptoms of you
And not anything else

I'd like to remain afflicted
Until my death

Pillows

Sometimes I have to set up pillows
And jump into them as hard as I can
As though I were hugging a person
After running at them from far away

And then I lay there
Hugging and hugging
And I start to cry

From the hopeful feeling
That I've escaped a hugless life

Drink Maker

Candle flame softens things
And drinks are made by lovely hands
Peeking from under sweater sleeves
That are practical but big

This person has done it all
And making you this is vacation

She walks with grace as on tippy toes
A type of body communication

She wants you to know that she loves you
With every movement she makes
And with every flavor
That she'll soon have you taste

And her eyes are fire
More warm than candle or drink itself

They desire you
To enjoy and to sip and to love

Freckle Color

Two freckles
By the mouth

One under the eye
And on the chin

Eyes are freckle color
And hair as well

Shedding brown
All over

Tumbled and moved
And touched often

Broom full of it
Like giant brush

I really like myself
The cleanup is worth it

I really like myself
And my freckle color

Inside Me

How can you call me beautiful
When I'm a giant person

I take up all the room
With all my emotion

I can hardly walk
From how much I love you

Do you want to live inside me
I think you're supposed to

It would solve so many problems
It'd put my size in proportion

Melted

Sleeping good after good fucking

Feet by feet
Hands on bodies
Hair all fanned out

Breasts enjoying the air
That's warm from touching

Two heaters together
That are us

Especially in winter
Deliciously so

We were like tongue
To each other's ice cream

But now we're melted
And it's good

Favorite Ingredient

I suck on you for nutrients

Sometimes I have you raw
Other times I mix you up with stuff

I take you different places
And see what you soak up

Observe your chemical reactions
Changes in flavor, texture, color

And replicate aspects
Cooking your love

I learn so much and feel so much
In my body and my mind and my soul

You are my favorite ingredient
You give me endorphins and love

Their House

Being woke up in the morning
To a breakfast I don't know

After cold feet through the nighttime
And wishing for my love

I can't even masturbate
As a guest in someone's home

When I wake, I pretend to be asleep
Until I have to pee enough to get up

And the floor is colder on my feet
Than the blankets were

And their soap doesn't smell like me
And makes my skin hurt

Yet all the same
I'm happy to be

And happy to be here

Glow

I've got a warmth on my body
Like a big winter coat
As comfortable as a sleeping bag
As mobile as skin

It's following me everywhere
So clothes are not needed

If I had known
I would not have spent money on them

It's as though I'm glowing
But invisibly so

I'd fear for my safety
If I didn't enjoy it so much

I'm not sure what is happening
But I think it is love

I don't think it matters
What I wear anymore

Let's Tunnel Away

We have tunneled to China
And now we're here

There are beautiful lanterns
And no more people with beards

There are dumplings on a platter
And I suck on their juice

And you watch me happily
As some trickles from my mouth
Onto my boobs

And there is no more clothing
As now we're in bed

And no more worrying
And only me
Giving you head

Feeling

My lips will hover over you
Just so you know I'm there

But I will not touch you
Though you'll feel the warmth all around

Every place my fingers linger
Right above your skin

Every breath
And every movement
And the anticipation I feel

And if you find yourself reeling
And moaning under your breath

And on the sheets, like a cat kneading
Balling them up in your hands

Then you'll know what I've been feeling
From a million miles away

Coming Closer

The moon is bigger than ever
Or so they say

I feel a déjà vu about it
Like there's a super moon every day

Is the moon crawling nearer
Across the sky to scoop me up

And take me someplace colder
Quieter
Where it's just us

Is the moon sending me a love letter
Through all my friends

Saying
You can't take my picture
And that makes me yours
More than anything you could

I'm here to hold you
Until your death

Staining Memories

Colors and colors
Fill it in between the lines

Pale ones and dark ones
Highlighting aspects of our minds

Turning into watercolor
Bleeding through time

Complimenting all the moments
Maintaining our vibe

Someday we'll be ancient
But as long as the pink in our skin
Stands out because of the red and white
In our clothes and in our lamp
And in its light and in our bed

We'll have with us this wonderful
Time that we now have

Like eating something flavorful
You did when you were a kid

Staining memories on purpose
But also by accident

Leaving little flower buds on them
Like wine on a shirt

And on our lips

Forever

Leading up to your love
And we are so close

Every day it seems more
Like it's already known

It's already there
Like you're inside my arms
And inside elsewhere
And of course
Inside my heart

I can feel my self-consciousness
Leaving forever

Any time it cries out
I know it's last gasps
Soon to be washed off
With soap and water

And then I'll be there
And none of it will matter

No more past
No more future

Only forever

Heartbeats

I am so lucky
For this experience

How many people get to touch themselves
For more than a few minutes
When horny alone

How many people get to
Reach in their heart
And rub it until
Something besides ache comes out

Aching and aching
For a very long time

Until the muscle is suddenly
At least no longer feeling
Like it's going to die

Feeling like
Heartbeats are noticed
One at a time

And breaths are noticed
And everything maybe
Will be alright

Bending Light

My hands are so beautiful
When I have my glasses on

The light bends different then
Narrow and delicate
Long and pointed
As though they're floating
And feel good to the touch

Soft and poreless
On your temples

Warm when you are cold
Cold when you are hot

That is how I'm used to
Seeing them as long as I remember

When I started to wear contacts
My face became more beautiful
But my fingers suffered

I wonder what they will look like
In the way your light bends

Maybe because you know they're mine
They'll look like them again

Hope

Are these love letters
To the world or to my friend

To my soulmate
To my lover
To my self
Whoever picked me up again

Did I come out crawling
From the places I've been

Like a sandwich on the floor
But still eatable and fresh

Will I be a deli
In some day I can't fathom

Where there's a whole bunch of me
Either through industry or children

Is that what I want
To be filled up with my taste

Fulfilled and appreciated and loved
By lines wrapping around the street

I can't know right now
Or expect anything

I'm just glad to exist
I'm glad to be something

Made in the USA
Middletown, DE
09 July 2024

57019440R00130